REGULAR EXP

I0011185

SIMPLICITY AND POWER IN CODE

DOUGLAS BERDEAUX

REGULAR EXPRESSIONS

SIMPLICITY AND POWER IN CODE, *1337th Edition*

Witten by Douglas Berdeaux
Copyright © 2013/2014 By WeakNet Laboratories
Printed by: Createspace in the United States
Editors: null
Cover Design: Douglas Berdeaux

WeakNet Laboratories: weaknetlabs.com
SquidBlackList: squidblacklist.org
Phone Losers of America: phonelosers.org
Hax Radio: haxradio.com

INDEX

Conventions used in this book

Monospace used for applications and shell output.

Chapter titles are large and bold

Subsections are a bit smaller and bold.

```
Shell:~$ output will be in monospace and inside of a single
table
-bash: output: command not found
```

Listings are *chapter.subsection.number* for easy recall

Regex matches from output will be highlighted

A regular expression is explained literally with this text style

'c'haracters *"strings"*

OR AND NOT LOGIC

Important terms are bold and italicized – so take notes!

Lulz are used when no one's looking

Preface

Whether it's for coding applications, writing scripts, parsing through CSV files, sanitizing user input, or even altering thousands of files at once, *Regular Expressions* are usually the best, most efficient option to complete the task. As a programmer, one of the first things I usually end up doing when learning a new language is looking for the functions and libraries that are used for searching and replacing using Regular Expression patterns.

One can really master the ins and outs of the GNU Linux kernel output and operating system configuration files using a few simple commands; each of which take Regular Expressions as arguments. I also use them on a daily basis each time I have to debug another coworker's code, saving me hours of chasing around variables and components in massive, multi-file applications.

As you read on, don't think of Regular Expressions as a shortcut, but as a sub-language. Think of them as a powerful basis for an efficient life and way of thinking. This guide won't make anyone a master at them; that actually takes some imagination, intuition and lots of practice. Making code and tasks simpler, tighter, more efficient, reliable and secure are what Regular Expressions excel with.

I will keep all examples as succinct as possible and by the time we are done, we won't have a need for a *"cheat sheet."* We will be working with simple GNU-Linux applications that come with most distributions. A lot of things that we *do* have to memorize for Regular Expressions are easy to remember. The language is so easy to use that after learning only a few special symbols, we'll be well on our way to minimizing the amount time it takes to complete tasks.

I will be using a lot of beginner examples and dialog for general shell commands. So if you are new to the subject, why not take a night or even weekend and follow along with the examples? You can dive right into a virtual machine using a live disk (I offer one free from my site) if you are not currently using Linux as your primary operating system. I don't recommend, however, using Microsoft Windows terminal emulators, as most of them come with half-assed versions of many Regular Expression powered applications – some of which require you to pay money for them! Also, I assume that we have prior knowledge of Perl for those interested in the Perl Regular Expressions chapters.

You can create your own files and regex patterns as you go along. In fact, it's best to go off on tangents and learning on your own with trial and error while reading through this hand book. Take your time and have fun or just read right though in an hour, it's up to you. The only real way to master Regular Expressions is through practice and consistency. I promise that this is a very powerful skill that when mastered, will open a massive amount of potential for programmers, system administrators and Linux hobbyists alike.

Douglas Berdeaux – 2014 *founder of WeakNet Laboratories*

I

Ex·pres·sion

/ik'spreSHən/ Noun

1. A finite combination of symbols that are well-formed according to the rules applicable in the context.

What are Regular Expressions?

Regular Expressions, *regexp*, *regex*, or just *RE* for short, are simple expressions, similar to the Algebra definition which are used when producing customized output. In fact, when comparing them to their Algebraic cousins, we can think of *meta-characters* as variables, *quantifiers* as operators, and *literal characters* and *strings* as constants using simple Algebra terminology. A meta-character has a special meaning to the application that is interpreting the Regular Expression pattern, or *interpreter* for short. By *expression*, we mean a set or pattern of well-formed symbols or characters. What do we mean by "*well-formed*?" Well, the characters must follow simple syntactical rules or they will be interpreted by the application using the expression as a literal string or just plain garbage. This is because some symbols within certain contexts are used as variables and modifiers, just like how a plus symbol '+' or minus symbol '-' are used to represent that we want to modify what's about to returned to us.

In the English language, we use capital letters to denote the beginning of a sentence or proper noun. Once we see a capital letter mid-sentence, we shift our mode of thinking to note that we are referring to a proper noun. If we use capital letters in the wrong places, the text would become confusing! We will be covering these special characters in section 3, but for now let's try a simple matching example.

```
^--?h(elp)?$
```

The above statement is our very first Regular Expression. This regexp, or *pattern*, states "*a line beginning with a hyphen (followed by a hyphen OR NOT followed by a hyphen) followed by an 'h' character, followed by the string "elp" OR NOT followed by the string "elp', then the end of the line.*" Don't worry too much about the special characters or syntax just yet because that's what the rest of this book is for! This regex can be used for command line arguments to scripts to see if the user is searching for help dialog with either "-h", "—help", or even "—h" and "-help" which makes our application immensely more flexible with much less code! If we write a script that accepts input and we want to check for all four of those strings ("-h","—help","—h","-help"), we would have to do a check on the input string 4 times. This actually happens in code that people or institutions have paid money to code or license! What if the user types "—foo"? Then, we could end up with undesired or *semantic errors* in our code or script. If we could check for all four of those, or even more with one, small, single line of code, we not only make our code easier to read, but more flexible, easier to maintain, and even easier to expand upon.

History and the Sets

By using the term *"regular,"* we hope that the Regular Expression language, or syntax, is universal and supported in the same manner throughout all programming languages and applications. The term *"regular"* comes from the original author, Stephen Cole Kleene, who in the 1950s described them using mathematical notation that he dubbed *"Regular Sets."* Unfortunately, we sometimes have to specify between a few different generations and families of Regular Expressions and sometimes we can even be extremely limited in what is available per family. This, of course, all depends on the Regular Expression interpreter application's author(s).

Our first generation of this family, or Simple Regular Expressions, were some of the first expressions ever used in computer science, around 1965 by Ken Thompson in the QED[1] text editor for searching for strings. This first generation was modified and amended to become our second generation known simply as *Basic Regular Expressions*, or BRE for short. In Basic Regular Expressions, we needed to escape certain meta-characters to tell the interpreter that they are

---

[1] UNIX "Quick Editor"

used as meta-characters and not their otherwise literal meaning. An example would be the opening parenthesis in the example above. Without specifying ERE in some applications, our Regular Expression pattern would be interpreted as a plain literal character '('. We would have needed to put a backslash in front of the parenthesis for the interpreter to know we are starting a set in our regex pattern. This is still the case in some applications including vim version 7.3.632 which is the latest at the time of writing this book. To use the latest generation of Regular Expressions (ERE) in vim, we must change the level what the authors call *"magic."* This is definitely not the case with the Perl programming language! In fact, Perl's Regular Expression support is so expansive and so well defined that Perl's Regular Expressions are known for being the "de-facto standard" today. (Wikipedia, 2013)

As time moves on, so do families. Our third generation of Regular Expressions is called **Extended Regular Expressions**, or ERE for short. A few quantifier meta-characters were added and the logic operator OR. A **quantifier** helps the applications developer to specify how many, or the quantity of matches he or she wants from the Regular Expressions.

```
[trevelyn@shell ~]$ grep '(lol)' file.txt
[trevelyn@shell ~]$ grep '\(lol\)' file.txt
this line has ("lol"); code
[trevelyn@shell ~]$ grep -E '(lol)' file.txt
this line has ("lol"); code
[trevelyn@shell ~]$
```

Listing 1.2.0: specifying ERE in modern grep with FreeBSD 9.1

In *listing 1.2.0* above, we can see that we need to tell grep to use ERE by passing the "-E" argument, or else it will only return lines that do not contain the literal string *"(lol)"*. If we *escape* the parenthesis with backslashes only then matches will occur. This is an easy way to tell if BRE is in use or not. If we do both and escape the parenthesis and specify we want to use ERE, we will get nothing returned by grep.

These families are all regulated by the IEEE[2] in a standards set of documents called *POSIX*, or <u>P</u>ortal <u>O</u>perating <u>S</u>ystem <u>I</u>nterface which defines many specifications for UNIX-like operating systems.

---

[2] <u>I</u>nstitute for <u>E</u>lectrical and <u>E</u>lectronic <u>E</u>ngineers.

So, where are Regular Expressions used?

Regular Expressions are used in more places than we may now. From search bars and form input sanitation in web applications with simple Javascript, to backend server-side code that performs data sorting and even database queries.

In the UNIX and GNU Linux operating systems, everything is made into a file. A large portion of these files are in plain text and used for configuration of system devices or applications. They can also be used to look at output from what a physically attached device is telling the kernel via drivers, e.g. the ACPI[3] modules in the newer GNU Linux kernel outputs battery data from our laptops to certain files within the /sys/class/ directory. If this is plain text, then we can write simple scripts and applications that can utilize that data very easily.

Parsing is the act of pulling out only the information that we need from a bunch of data. Data is only data until we change it into information by giving it meaning. We parse out words like "battery power: " to get only the numerical value used after the string to display the power for our own scripts. Sometimes this becomes more advanced, like when we get a millisecond value from a time-clock device in /dev/. We need to perform simple mathematics on the millisecond value to change it into a more human readable form, like seconds. These are just a few simple examples of a vast potential for script writing in GNU Linux. Mostly all parsing in GNU Linux, if in shell scripts or system calls from programming languages, can be easily done using *AWK*, *sed*, and *grep* - each of which can take Regular Expressions as arguments.

---

[3] Advance Power and Configuration Interface that allows the GNU Linux kernel to control your power settings.

GREP

Let's begin with grep since we already had an example with it. If we want to search a file in a UNIX or UNIX-like operating system for a particular character or any specifically ordered group of characters, sometimes referred to as a *string*, we usually have the option of using pre-installed applications like grep to do the job. grep stands for <u>G</u>lobal <u>R</u>egular <u>E</u>xpression <u>P</u>rint/<u>P</u>arse and we have yet to come across a version of a UNIX-like operating system that lacks it in a default installation. It searches a file character by character filtering for the string or expression that we provide.

If we pass a single character or a string to grep it will return any line in which that character or string exists and filter out the rest. For instance, if we want to print all lines in a text file with the word *"foo"*, we can do so, just as we do in *listing 2.1.0*.

```
[trevelyn@shell ~/regex]$ grep foo file.txt
foo
food for thought
foofoofoofoo
[trevelyn@shell ~/regex]$
```

Listing 2.1.0: Using grep *in its simplest of forms.*

grep, like many Linux commands and UNIX file systems, is case sensitive. We can make our searches case *in*-sensitive by passing the '-i' argument to grep. We can also negate our searches by passing the '-v' argument and print out all of the lines that would normally be filtered out, displaying only those that <u>do not</u> match our regexp.

```
[trevelyn@shell ~/regex]$ cat file.txt
this line has no f-o-o occurrence
this line contains foo
abcdefghijklmnop
qrstuvwxyz123456
[trevelyn@shell ~/regex]$ grep -v foo file.txt
this line has no f-o-o occurrence
abcdefghijklmnop
qrstuvwxyz123456
[trevelyn@shell ~/regex]$ grep foo file.txt
this line contains foo
[trevelyn@shell ~/regex]$ grep d file.txt
abcdefghijklmnop
[trevelyn@shell ~/regex]$ grep 3 file.txt
qrstuvwxyz123456
[trevelyn@shell ~/regex]$
```

Listing 2.1.1: A few grep filter examples.

In *listing 2.1.1*, we see a few examples of how grep filters the output of the file to match only what we specify it to. The command cat simply displays the entire file to our screen once and exits. In our second command we say to filter out all occurrences of the word, or string, "*foo*" using the '-v' argument. There is a vast amount of arguments we can pass to grep as it is an extremely comprehensive text filtering application.

We must be careful for what we search for in grep because, by default grep actually listens for special characters used in Regular Expression syntax. We will learn more about these special characters, called meta-characters, later on.

```
[trevelyn@shell ~/regex]$ grep -n . file.txt
1:this line has a carat ^ right in the middle.
2:this line has no carat.
[trevelyn@shell ~/regex]$ grep -n ^ file.txt
1:this line has a carat ^ right in the middle.
2:this line has no carat.
[trevelyn@shell ~/regex]$ grep -nF ^ file.txt
1:this line has a carat ^ right in the middle.
[trevelyn@shell ~/regex]$ grep -n \\^ file.txt
1:this line has a carat ^ right in the middle.
[trevelyn@shell ~/regex]$ grep -n no file.txt
2:this line has no carat.
[trevelyn@shell ~/regex]$
```

Listing 2.1.2: a meta-character search causes unintentional output.

In *listing 2.1.2*, we first display all lines that contain a character. Then in the second example we see that the carat character '^' was matched in both lines, yet the second line doesn't even contain one! This is because it is a special character used in Regular Expression syntax and once grep notices one, it thinks that we are trying to match the beginning of a line (which technically both lines have a beginning so they both match and are returned). We have to escape the character, or pass the "–F" argument which makes grep treat our character as just a simple character and nothing else as we do in the third example. We also learn than passing the "-n" argument shows what line number the match occurred on. This is can be very useful for source code debugging outside of an integrated development environment. This is proved when we pass the string "*no*" to grep and we match "*no*" only in the second line which is labeled with a '2'.

grep is an incredible text filter application and is good for searching and filtering through giant-sized log and configuration files, HTML parsing, and even used for source code debugging among a seemingly infinite amount of possibilities!

AWK

grep is more than amazing for returning entire lines, but what if we have a column-like, or comma separated output and want to show only one particular column or field without adding extra syntax to our script or application? Maybe we need to show just one matched word in a whole sentence of words. For these tasks, we can use **AWK**.[4] AWK stands for Alfred <u>A</u>ho, Peter <u>W</u>einberger, and Brian <u>K</u>ernighan, which are the application author's collective surname initials. AWK is actually a full-blown, powerful programming language with its own logic and keywords that can be used to display output from files and other applications, split up and substitute lines and characters from output, make system calls to run commands, read and parse multiple files at once in unison and much more. When mastered, AWK and Regular Expressions amass to one of the most powerful and efficient tools in UNIX-like operating systems. Here we will only cover how to split up lines, and very little of the language itself. It is very powerful and we recommend any one reading who is unfamiliar with AWK to do a little research and get familiarized with it.[5]

```
[trevelyn@shell ~/regex]$ awk '{if ($0 ~ /foo/)  print $0}'
file.txt
foo is not foo
foo multi-column-foo-example foo
food for thought
foofoofoofoo
[trevelyn@shell ~/regex]$ awk '{if ($0 ~ /foo/)  print $2}'
file.txt
is
multi-column-foo-example
for
[trevelyn@shell ~/regex]$ awk '$0 ~ /foo/{print $0}' file.txt
foo is not foo
foo multi-column-foo-example foo
food for thought
foofoofoofoo
[trevelyn@shell ~/regex]$
```
Listing 2.2.0: Using AWK in its simplest of forms.

In *listing 2.2.0* above, we first use AWK and say "*if the entire line contains the string occurrence "foo" then print the entire line*" –

---

[4] Or sed, if we just truncate all of the garbage data with special Regular Expressions.

[5] It's a *huge* time saver with tasks with columned output like "ps"

which AWK denotes with a sigil and integer to $0.[6] We use an `if` statement and have our *clause* in parenthesis. If the clause returns true, then the code in the curly-braces, called a **block of code**, or **compound statement**, will run – which in our case prints the entire line. Then, we call the same command again, but this time we tell AWK to print only column 2 from the line, as AWK denotes column 2 as $2 and we have made column 2 grey in the first example. After which, we pass the file name at the end of the command to search and display from. Without the filename, AWK, `sed` and `grep` will wait for input from **STDIN** or "Standard Input" – which is most likely our keyboard.

In our final command in *listing 2.2.0*, we use a shorthand notation for `if` statement syntax. There are no parenthesis needed and the code in the block will still run, since the clause: *"if the whole line ($0) contains the string "foo""* before the block evaluates to true.

We can also change the **delimiter,** or separator. By default, AWK uses the field separator as any whitespace. So in *listing 2.2.0*, the lines are split by spaces. If we pass the "-F" argument to AWK, we can specify anything else, including commas for CSV[7] files just as we see in *listing 2.2.1*. Not only do we change the delimiter to '-', ',', and it's default, which is space, but we also use a regex pattern!

---

[6] Column 1 is $1, column 2 is $2, etc... but don't forget if you want the line you can just use "print" or $0!

[7] Comma-separated files, where each field is separated by a comma.

```
[trevelyn@shell ~/regex]$ awk '{print $0}' file.txt
this line has space
this,line,is,comma,separated
this-line-is-hyphen-separated
[trevelyn@shell ~/regex]$ awk '{print $1}' file.txt
this
this,line,is,comma,separated
this-line-is-hyphen-separated
[trevelyn@shell ~/regex]$ awk -F, '{print $1}' file.txt
this line has space
this
this-line-is-hyphen-separated
[trevelyn@shell ~/regex]$ awk -F'-' '{print $1}' file.txt
this line has space
this,line,is,comma,separated
this
[trevelyn@shell ~/regex]$ awk '{print $0}' file.txt
this line has space
this,line,is,comma,separated
this,line,is,coma,separated
this-line-is-hyphen-separated
[trevelyn@shell ~/regex]$ awk -F'comm?a' '{print $1}'
file.txt
this line has space
this,line,is,
this,line,is,
this-line-is-hyphen-separated
[trevelyn@shell ~/regex]$
```

Listing 2.2.1: changing the field separator value from spaces to command and hyphen and even a regexp pattern.

Everything between the forward slashes is interpreted as a Regular Expression in AWK, unless it is a variable when using the syntax for AWK programming.[8] The tilde '~' means "*contains*" and that expression is in parenthesis similar to other programming and scripting languages. Once AWK finds a line that contains the sequence of characters 'f','o', and 'o' it returns true and the line or column specified is then printed to **STDOUT,** or "Standard Output" – which is usually the terminal displayed on our screen. AWK can do *much* more than this and is a great ally when working with UNIX-like operating systems.

---

[8] AWK variables are not interpolated, resolved, or dereferenced, when used in Regular Expression patterns.

```
[trevelyn@shell ~/regex]$ awk 'BEGIN {a="y"} /e/ {print $0}'
file.txt
this line has space
[trevelyn@shell ~/regex]$ awk 'BEGIN {a="y"} /e/ {print a}'
file.txt
y
y
y
[trevelyn@shell ~/regex]$
```

Listing 2.2.2 AWK does not resolve what 'a' points to

In *listing 2.2.2*, we see that AWK treats everything that is not a simple Regular Expression meta-character as a literal constant. Here we see that the character 'a' is just an 'a' and nothing else even after we assign it as a variable to the character 'y'. If we wanted to search for the value of our variable, we could just use a tilde '~'[9] and a single variable name without forward slashes, or use the built in match() function in AWK just like our first command in *listing 2.2.3*.

```
[trevelyn@shell ~/regex]$ awk 'BEGIN {a="y"} match($0,a)
{print $0,"has a y"}' file.txt
this-line-is-hyphen-separated has a y
[trevelyn@shell ~/regex]$ awk 'BEGIN {a="y"} $0 ~ a {print
$0,"has a y"}' file.txt
this-line-is-hyphen-separated has a y
```

Listing 2.2.3: AWK's match() function and simple tilde search using a variable.

SED

Now let's talk about string and character substitution. As with the factory-standard applications, grep and AWK,[10] we have another commonly pre-installed application for this process called sed. sed stands for **S**tream **Ed**itor. It was influenced by an ancient line-by-line text editor named ed. It too, has a set of commands and can be used as a scripting language like its cousin AWK. If we have a script that requires the output of a file to be altered to work properly we can do so with

---

[9] This can be negated by adding a simple '!' in front of the tilde, exactly like Perl's matching operator. 0 !~ a

[10] AWK actually has sed functionality built into it, minus the back referencing (which are available in gawk) with functions like sub(); and gsub();

sed. We can also alter[11] the file without even opening it.[12] In fact, we can alter thousands of files, all at once without even opening them to our screen!

```
[trevelyn@shell ~/regex]$ grep foo file.txt | sed 's/foo/bar/'
bar is not foo
bar multi-column-foo-example foo
bard for thought
barfoofoo
[trevelyn@shell ~/regex]$
```

Listing 2.3.0: using sed *to substitute the string "foo" with "bar"*

In *listing 2.3.0* above, we used both grep and sed together. First, grep printed us the lines that contained the string "*foo*". Then we pipe the output, using the special shell character '|' which hands off the output of grep to the next command sed. sed's argument 's/foo/bar/' is pretty easy syntax. Let's break this command up into four parts using the '/' as a delimiter.

```
sed 'command/regex pattern/string/modifier'
```

The 's' in *listing 2.3.0* means that sed will be running a *substitution command*. The next character '/' is then interpreted by sed as the delimiter[13] to the command which can actually be any other printable character. sed then saves all characters after the first delimiter until it sees another delimiter character, in our case a '/', saving "*foo*". This means, when dealing with strings we should be careful as to what delimiter character we choose. If it sees another delimiter character, sed then begins reading in the next set of characters "*bar*" which becomes the string we use to replace the first string "*foo*" with. Once the last delimiter is reached, sed then interprets the last character as a modifier, if one exists. A modifier such as 'g' can be used to globally change *all* occurrences of "*foo*" to "*bar*." We can also specify which occurrence we

---

[11] Sed actually overwrites the file with the new modified version when using the "-i" option

[12] "opening" meaning printing to STDOUT

[13] A delimiter is a separator character, similar to how a comma ',' in a CSV file separates the fields

want to change by prepending an integer to the 'g'. As we see in *listing 2.3.0*, we only changed the first occurrence. When applied in *listing 2.3.1*, we change all occurrences.

```
[trevelyn@shell ~/regex]$ cat file.txt
foo the foo bar baz!
barred to baz the foo food
foolishly, food at the store "thefoodstore" isn't great.
[trevelyn@shell ~/regex]$ sed 's/foo/bar/' file.txt
bar the foo bar baz!
barred to baz the bar food
barlishly, food at the store "thefoodstore" isn't great.
[trevelyn@shell ~/regex]$ sed 's/foo/bar/g' file.txt
bar the bar bar baz!
barred to baz the bar bard
barlishly, bard at the store "thebardstore" isn't great.
[trevelyn@shell ~/regex]$
```

Listing 2.3.1: using the 'g' global modifier.

We can make our `sed` command interpret our Regular Expressions or string without case sensitivity as well. If we attach a simple 'i' at the end of the expression command, e.g. 's/FOO/BAR/i' `sed` will change all occurrences of "*foo*" or "*FOO*" or even "*FoO*" into "*BAR*." We can also use several modifiers at once, like changing all occurrences and ignoring case.

All three applications we just covered utilize Regular Expressions. Anything between the first set of forward slashes of the substitution command (in our case "*foo*") gets interpreted as a regex. "*foo*" is, in fact, a regex pattern where each character matches itself. Sometimes we need to specify to AWK, `sed` and `grep` that we are going to be using Regular Expressions, Extended Regular Expressions, or Perl Regular Expressions with a simple argument, e.g. "-r" to `sed` in GNU Linux. This whole time we just simply used the string "*foo*" as our expression.

Where Else Are They Used?

Very few programming languages and applications offer little or no Regular Expression support. Many programmers accept Regular Expressions from the user without even realizing it. An example would be a Perl script that takes input and searches a string in a file for the input. If the search function were coded as if($_ =~ m/$ARGV[0]/) The first argument sent to the Perl script from the user, which Perl denotes as the first list item in the array @ARG, can be in the form "*f.o*" ,"*foo*",".*o*.", or ".*oo*" and still match all occurrences of "*foo*" because Perl will compile it as a Regular Expression! This is because Perl will compile everything between forward slashes into a regex pattern. The "=~" syntax (slightly similar to AWK) means "*contains*."

Some newer versions of applications are widely used as well, such as extended-grep or egrep (which is similar to grep with "-E" set as default) and GNU-AWK or gawk.

Note!
Some applications require that you pass an argument to them to let them know you want to use Extended Regular Expressions. If you don't you may not get your desired output!

Language /application	Methods or functions			
Coldfusion	REReplace	REFind	REMatch	
PHP (PCRE)	preg_match	preg_replace	preg_filter	preg_grep
Perl	s/regexp/string/	m/regexp/	grep(/regexp/, @array)	
Javascript	str.replace(regexp string);	str.match(/regexp/)		
Vim	s/regexp/string/	/regexp		
Java	str.matches	str.split	str.replace	
Oracle SQL	REGEXP_LIKE(column,'re gexp')	REGEXP_REPLACE(column, 'regexp','replacement')		
MySQL	REGEX			

Table 2.4.0: A listing of a very few applications and languages that support Regular Expressions. A few examples can be found in final chapter of this book.

II

Syn·tax

/'sin,taks/ Noun

2. The arrangement of words and phrases to create well-formed sentences in a language.

Characters, Meta-characters and String Matching

Now that we know how these applications work, let's begin with Regular Expression syntax. We will begin with a simple variable, or meta-character, '.' The period, in Regular Expression syntax, literally means "*any character.*" So a Regular Expression "*fo.*" will match "*foo*","*fo1*","*fof*","*fo_*","*fo+*","*foX*", ... ,"*fo* " (that's a space) and so on. *Meta-character* simply means that '.' has a special meaning to the *interpreter* of the regex pattern (Perl, sed, AWK, grep, ... , etc). There are quite a few others, such as '^','$','|','[',']','(',')', and compound characters that are escaped such as "\d" which means "*any digit starting with 0 through and including 9*" and "\w" which means "*any word character*"

```
[trevelyn@shell ~/regex]$ egrep buthasan file.txt
thislinehasnospacesbecausespacesarebadbuthasan!
thislinehasnospacesbecausespacesarebadbuthasan@
thislinehasnospacesbecausespacesarebadbuthasan()
thislinehasnospacesbecausespacesarebadbuthasan*
thislinehasnospacesbecausespacesarebadbuthasan_
thislinehasnospacesbecausespacesarebadbuthasan-
thislinehasnospacesbecausespacesarebadbuthasan.
[trevelyn@shell ~/regex]$ egrep buthasan file.txt | egrep
'\W'
thislinehasnospacesbecausespacesarebadbuthasan!
thislinehasnospacesbecausespacesarebadbuthasan@
thislinehasnospacesbecausespacesarebadbuthasan()
thislinehasnospacesbecausespacesarebadbuthasan*
thislinehasnospacesbecausespacesarebadbuthasan-
thislinehasnospacesbecausespacesarebadbuthasan.
[trevelyn@shell ~/regex]$
```

Listing 3.1.0: we use the non-word meta-character in the second command and see that "_" was omitted.

In *listing 3.1.0*, we passed a literal string to egrep, which it will interpret as a string or "*buthasan*". We also see that the meta-character '_' was omitted in the second command. This is because the characters

'A' through 'Z' and 'a' through 'z'[14] and '_' are considered "*word*" characters. The escaped capital "\W" negates the filter for word-characters. If we also capitalize "\d" or "*any digit*" to be "\D" we negate the statement and mean "*any non-digit character.*" There are a few other meta-characters that we can capitalize to negate them. These initials are very easy to remember, and it's also easy to remember to capitalize them if we don't want them! Another set of commonly used meta-characters we should familiarize ourselves with are the non-printable characters that include "\a", "\r", "\n", "\v". They stand for a system bell, carriage return, newline and TAB key, respectively. The system bell will cause the terminal to beep or blink if the pcspkr GNU Linux kernel module is in use. The carriage return is used to return back to the start of the current line, the new-line is similar to simply hitting enter and the TAB key is used for indentation in formal writing and programming.

Another useful compound meta-character is for matching any white space. **Whitespace** can come from hitting the spacebar or TAB keys. Can you guess what initial is used before looking? It's "\s" (for 's'pace maybe?). Simple enough to not even need a cheat sheet! If we want any non-space character in a match how do you think we would represent that negation? You've (probably) guessed it! "\S"

```
[trevelyn@shell ~/regex]$ grep '\S' file.txt
[trevelyn@shell ~/regex]$ grep -E '\S' file.txt
[trevelyn@shell ~/regex]$ grep -E -e '\S' file.txt
[trevelyn@shell ~/regex]$ egrep -E -e '\S' file.txt
[trevelyn@shell ~/regex]$ egrep -E '\S' file.txt
[trevelyn@shell ~/regex]$ egrep '\S' file.txt
[trevelyn@shell ~/regex]$ cat file.txt
this contains spaces
thisdoesnotcontainspaces
[trevelyn@shell ~/regex]$ grep -V
grep (GNU grep) 2.5.1-FreeBSD
```

Listing 3.1.1: GNU grep in FreeBSD doesn't recognize the meta-character \S'

---

[14] In computer science all characters have different base values or hexadecimal representation codes. So capital "A" (42) is literally different to a computer than lowercase "a" (61), just as in writing, so we expressed both in the example.

```
root@wt4blue:~# cat file.txt
this contains spaces
thisdoesnotcontainspaces
root@wt4blue:~# grep '\Sco' file.txt
thisdoesnotcontainspaces
root@wt4blue:~# grep '\s' file.txt
this contains spaces
root@wt4blue:~# grep -V
GNU grep 2.6.3
```

Listing 3.1.2: GNU grep in GNU Linux recognizes the meta-character '\S'

In the above two listings (*3.1.1* and *3.1.2*) we can see the differences between FreeBSD grep 2.5.1 and GNU Linux grep 2.6.3. One recognizes the meta-character "\S" the other does not. In fact, in the man page for FreeBSD grep, it states that we cannot use the Perl regular Expressions.

```
    -P, --perl-regexp        Interpret PATTERN as a Perl
regular expression.  This option is not supported in FreeBSD.
```

Listing 3.1.3: FreeBSD is one of many Operating Systems to come with pre-compiled and specially configured grep.

This is where most of us will have issues with trying to match strings: different versions of the same application across different platforms! We can however put an actual space in out regex pattern like so:

```
grep -E ' ' file.txt
```

Other spaces, like TAB on the other hand, will be interpreted by most modern shells for auto completion and "\v" just won't work if "\s" does not. Sometimes, a space ' ' will also match a TAB when using grep. If you believe that your Regular Expression syntax is correct, double check the manual page from your application!

```
[trevelyn@shell ~/regex]$ cat file.txt
terminal is nice
terminal is garbage
[trevelyn@shell ~/regex]$ grep '(c|g)' file.txt
[trevelyn@shell ~/regex]$ grep -E '(c|g)' file.txt
terminal is nice
terminal is garbage
[trevelyn@shell ~/regex]$ grep -E '(J|g)' file.txt
terminal is garbage
[trevelyn@shell ~/regex]$
```

Listing 3.1.4: Another example to which we need to pass '-E' to grep to show that we are using an "extended Regular Expression"

The example in *listing 3.1.4* shows that a basic Regular Expression differs from an extended in GNU grep version 2.6 in FreeBSD albeit the man-page offers this advice: "**grep** *understands two different versions of regular expression syntax: "basic" and "extended." In GNU* **grep***, there is no difference in available functionality using either syntax.*"

Another set of great meta-characters are the anchors. Anchors anchor your match to the beginning or end of line. The beginning of the line anchor is the '^' character. So a Regular Expression like "^abc" literally means *"the beginning of the line followed by an 'a' followed by a 'b' followed by a 'c'."*
This Regular Expression will match the following lines,

```
abc
abcd
abcde
abcd7632547263542342;3fljerlkhfweriuvh23iprncv3iodm31iomcoin
```

because they all follow the rule of our Regular Expression pattern. Now, what if we want to match the end of a line? That anchor is a dollar symbol '$'. A Regular Expression like "*okay\.$*" literally means "*an 'o' then 'k' then 'a' then 'y' then period then end line.*" This Regular Expression will match the following lines,

```
you will be okay.
You will learn Regular Expressions, okay.
Everything will soon be all over. You will be okay.
```

because they all follow the rules of our Regular Expression. Note that in this example expression we escaped the period with a backslash.

Without this backslash the period would be interpreted as the "*any character*" variable we mentioned in the beginning of this section. It would certainly still match our line since a period, technically is an "any character" but by escaping the character by prepending a backslash, we basically turn off this special meaning to match just a period. This way, a line ending with "*okayy*" would not match.

Strings and Words

We must be careful when trying to match strings as they are treated literally as groups of characters. Regular Expression patterns are usually interpreted character by character from left to right. Just as in basic Algebra, we can group together characters into a string using parenthesis, or not. An Algebraic example would be

```
(n*m+b)²
```

Math listing 3.2.0: a simple Algebraic expression with a unary superscript '2' modifying the entire statement

The expression above will be interpreted in the parenthesis first. Then the entire answer will be squared. We have grouped together "*n*m+b*" and can do so in just the same manner in Regular Expressions with characters to create strings. In *listing 3.1.4*, we drew parenthesis around the 'g' and 'c' characters. Our Algebraic expression above would return a totally different result if we remove the parenthesis and have:

```
N*m+b²
```

Math listing 3.2.1: a simple Algebraic expression with a unary superscript '2' only modifying 'b'

So we see that strings *must* be in a specific order. Regular Expression interpreters work in the same fashion, from left to right. We could use parenthesis to specify strings in regex like so:

```
(string1)
```

We don't always need the parenthesis, but this would allow us to use quantifier modifiers on the entire string and not just the '1' digit on the end, just as the exponent '2' in our Algebraic expression in *listing 3.2.0-3.2.1* showed us. This is because a string is simply just an ordered set of characters. There are two easy ways to group sets of characters in Regular Expressions and the second way using square brackets [] is an "*unordered*" set using <u>OR</u> logic, whereas the parenthesis we used earlier are an "*ordered*" set using <u>AND</u> logic exactly in the sequence to which they are passed.

Logic

Like Regular Expressions, Boolean logic is also derived from a subset of Algebra named after George Boole. It is a binary system which simply dictates that check and tried values can only resolve to *true* or *false*. The operators used are the **conjunction**, **disjunction** and **negation** operators named <u>AND</u>, <u>OR</u>, and <u>NOT</u> respectively. It's used very heavily in computer science for circuitry, programming and more.

Boolean <u>OR</u> Logic

Let's begin our section on logic with the Boolean logic operator <u>OR</u>. Just as any programming language, Regular Expression syntax has a special symbol for Boolean <u>OR</u> Logic. This is the pipe character '|' just like in *listing 3.1.4*. In Programming, we usually use two pipes for the logical operator "<u>OR</u>".

```
If(a == 0 || a == 3){
        return;
}
```

Code Listing 4.1.0: C programing using the logical OR operator, stating if variable "a" equals "0" or "3" then return from the function.

In *code listing 4.1.0*, we can see a simple logical <u>OR</u> operator being using in C programming. If the (hopefully integer) variable 'a' equals zero <u>OR</u> three, then the expression within the parenthesis is *true* and we return from the routine. If not, the expression is *false* and the block of code which tells the CPU to return from the routine within the curly braces is not run. We can do the same logic with Regular Expressions using the same character '|' In *listing 3.1.4*, we said "*if the line contained a character 'c' <u>OR</u> a 'g' then show us those lines.*" This finally produced output when we passed the '-E' for Extended Regular Expressions and it showed both lines because of the characters in the words "*garbage*" and "*nice.*" Now, Terminals can't really be both nice and garbage, so we altered our Regular Expression to be "*either a 'J' <u>OR</u> a 'g'*" and learned that terminal is "*garbage*" since a 'J' doesn't exist anywhere in either line.

Another way we can use <u>OR</u> logic is by using square brackets '[]'. When we place characters into square brackets in our regex pattern, we create a *set* or *class*. The set syntax [fb] in *listing 4.1.0* shows a set of only two characters, 'f' and 'b'. *Ranges* of characters are a short-hand way of specifying a set and can be denoted with a hyphen in Regular Expressions if used in square brackets. We can specify a range of characters in Boolean <u>OR</u> fashion like F-O[15] which literally means 'F' <u>OR</u> 'G' <u>OR</u> 'H' <u>OR</u> ... 'O', or simply "*'F' through 'O'*". If we wanted to search for F <u>OR</u> G <u>OR</u> H <u>OR</u> I <u>OR</u> J <u>OR</u> K <u>OR</u> L <u>OR</u> M <u>OR</u> N <u>OR</u> O we can type [FGHIJKLMNO] or the shorthanded range way with the hyphen [F-O]. A good example is when searching for a hexadecimal value which can include A through F, [A-F]

```
[trevelyn@shell ~/regex]$ grep -E '[fb]' file.txt
terminal is garbage
[trevelyn@shell ~/regex]$
```
Listing 4.1.0: OR logic being used with the set "f", "b" in the square brackets.

In *listing 4.1.0*, we can see that the line is returned even if grep didn't find an 'f'. This is because we are using basic OR logic. "*Match either an 'f' <u>OR</u> a 'b'.*" Since the square brackets specify unordered lists, we could have also specified [bf] and still received the same output. grep will check every single character per line for either an 'f' or a 'b'.

Note!
 Using the "-" for a shorthanded range expression cannot go backwards. Because each character on our screen is represented by an integer, we can only go forward with our ranges, e.g. 0-9, 4-11, 21-22. We cannot use a smaller number as the range end or we will get an error with an invalid range end message, e.g. 0-9, 11-4, 22-21.

```
[trevelyn@shell ~/regex]$ cat file.txt
very strange string
a big calf
[trevelyn@shell ~/regex]$ grep -E '[n-z]' file.txt
very strange string
[trevelyn@shell ~/regex]$
```

---

[15] That's a capital letter 'O'

Listing 4.1.1: the range operator "-" used with the grouping operators "[]"

In *listing 4.1.1*, we see another example of the range operator being used in square brackets that returns only the string which *contains the characters 'n' through 'z'* We can also specify more than one range in the square brackets. Say we want all upper case letters from A-F and all numbers from 0-9 to match hexadecimal representations. We can do so simply by putting both classes together into square brackets #[0-9a-fA-F]. This can return #000000 through #ffffff. Again, since these are unordered sets that don't need to be in any specific order and are tested with <u>OR</u> logic, so we can swap the classes and also say #[A-Fa-f0-9]. Remember, that depending on what interpreter we are using we can shorten this code by omitting the lowercase a-f range and using the 'i' case-insensitive search.

Another thing to note is that special meta-characters lose all meaning in square brackets, except for the backslash anywhere in the expression or a carat '^' if placed at the beginning of the inner expression. This means that the special meta-character period '.' literally means '.' and nothing more in a set. In fact, we can even throw in more square brackets like [][] this will attempt to match ']' and '['. If we want to add a hyphen to our collection, we can add it at the end to trick the interpreter into not thinking we are trying to specify another range like so: [0-9a-zA-Z._-].

Note!

When we are searching for the hyphen, '-', with other characters in a set, make sure to put the hyphen at the end of the expression like so:

```
[AsDd64GgH.-]
```

This way, our regex interpreter doesn't assume we are specifying another range!

All of these examples are fine for characters, but if we want to search for strings that contain words using <u>OR</u> logic in Regular

Expressions we can do so by delimiting them with a pipe and surrounding them with parenthesis as we do in *listing 4.1.2.*

```
[trevelyn@shell ~/regex]$ cat file.txt
Bobby called his mother "Pajama Pants"
Poppy sleeps all the time and is a model
Lavender loves Skittles
Twinkle hates when we flop around
Russell and Strawberry sitting in a tree
[trevelyn@shell ~/regex]$ grep -E '(sleeps|tree|loves)'
file.txt
Poppy sleeps all the time and is a model
Lavender loves Skittles
Russell and Strawberry sitting in a tree
[trevelyn@shell ~/regex]$
```

Listing 4.1.2: Using OR logic to display lines from files that contain only the strings we specify.

Boolean NOT Logic

Let's now take a look at Boolean <u>NOT</u> logic. Another thing we can do with ranges and sets is negating a character match with a carat, '^'. This symbol, when placed at the beginning of a set, or class, negates all characters in the set.

[^abc]

The above expression will match anything that is Boolean NOT 'a' NOT 'b' NOT 'c'. Note that lines that do contain these characters and other characters not within our set will still be printed. Here is an example:

```
[trevelyn@shell ~/regex]$ grep '[C]' file.txt
Camo and Krooked
[trevelyn@shell ~/regex]$ grep '[^C]' file.txt
Arkasia
Evol Intent
Camo and Krooked
[trevelyn@shell ~/regex]$
```

Listing 4.2.0: Negating a character doesn't mean negating the string!

In *listing 4.2.0*, we see that when specifying only one character in a range, only one result is returned. Yet, if we negate that to a Boolean <u>NOT</u>, all three lines in the file are returned even though our third line has a capital 'C'. This is because the line that does contain the 'C' as we specified also contains characters that are not 'C' and the entire line is checked character by character. If the file were to have just one character per line, 'A', 'B', 'C', then the 'A' and 'B' will be returned and the 'C' line will be ignored.

If we added a '^' carat to the expression outside of the square brackets, like so ^[^C] this would have anchored our match to the beginning of the line and the third result would not have been returned. This would literally mean *"any line that starts with any character that is <u>NOT</u> a capital 'C'."*

We cannot negate strings or single out characters in sentences or strings in Regular Expressions outside of using Perl's negated look-around (look-ahead or look-behind) and grep's very convenient "-v" argument. For the look-around syntax please see the Perl Regular Expression chapter.

Boolean AND Logic

Finally we are brought to the <u>AND</u> logic. When we think of strings, we can consider them to be what they literally are, and that is a set of characters in a specific sequence, or order. When a lone string is passed to the Regular Expression interpreter, it is interpreted as an ordered set using <u>AND</u> logic. For example, let's use the string *"rabbit."* To pass *"rabbit"* as a regex string, we surround it in parenthesis[16] "(rabbit)". Now, our interpreter will go character by character to match the string as 'r' <u>AND</u> then 'a' <u>AND</u> then 'b' <u>AND</u> then 'b' <u>AND</u> then 'i' <u>AND</u> then 't'. This is how we can use <u>AND</u> logic in Regular Expressions.

We can search for multiple strings as well using the any character meta-character '.' and a quantifier.

---

[16] Only necessary when using modifiers on the string, but good practice!

```
[trevelyn@shell ~/regex]$ cat file.txt
Bobby called his mother "Pajama Pants"
Poppy sleeps all the time and is a model
Lavender loves Skittles
Twinkle hates when we flop around
Russell and Strawberry sitting in a tree
[trevelyn@shell ~/regex]$ grep -E '(sleeps).*(model)'
file.txt
Poppy sleeps all the time and is a model
[trevelyn@shell ~/regex]$ grep -E 'Twi.*we.*around' file.txt
Twinkle hates when we flop around
[trevelyn@shell ~/regex]$
```

Listing 4.3.0 searching for multiple strings using Boolean AND logic.

In *listing 4.3.0* we used Boolean <u>AND</u> logic in our Regular Expression pattern to display lines that contain several strings at once using special characters called quantifiers.

Quantifier Syntax

Quantifier operators in Regular Expressions are similar to unary operators in mathematics and programming languages. They only operate on one single operand or token, which we can say is a string or character. They indicate to the regex interpreter that we want a specific amount of the previous object.

Not a Glob!

If you are familiar with GNU Linux's command line arguments that could contain a *"glob"* operator '*' to mean *"anything"* (e.g. `rm -rf /tmp/lol/*`), then you already know that the asterisk is a special character to the shell. This is not used in the same way in Regular Expressions. Here it is a quantifier operator that just means *"any amount of the previous character or grouped expression."* This is where DOS and other shell users may stumble and get confused when dealing with the regex meaning of the asterisk. It itself is not a variable, but a **quantifier** for a variable or literal. The asterisk doesn't do anything but a quantity: *"zero or many of the previous match."* The match could be a string, set, or a single character. Its syntax rules are similar to the exponent symbol in *math listing 3.2.0* and alters the previous character or string in parenthesis.

```
[trevelyn@shell ~/regex]$ grep -E 'Z*' file.txt
very strange string
a big calf
[trevelyn@shell ~/regex]$
```

*Listing 5.1.0: The * quantifier being used impractically.*

In *Listing 5.1.0* above, we see that we got results back when we don't even have a capital 'Z' in any of the strings! Well, this is because the '*' quantifier literally means *"zero OR as many as you give me of the previous character."* And since we do, in fact, have zero 'Z's, we get both results.

```
[trevelyn@shell ~/regex]$ grep -E 'bi*g' file.txt
a big calf
[trevelyn@shell ~/regex]$
```

Listing 5.1.1: the "*" quantifier used a little better!

In *Listing 5.1.1*, we can see the "***" quantifier operator used a little better than before and that our Regular Expression clearly states *"match a 'b' with zero or more 'i's then a 'g'"* This would match the strings "*bg*", "*big*", "*biig*", "*biiig*", "*biiiig*", etc.

If we want to specify a string and say *"zero or more occurrences of the string "thisString""* we can do so by simply using parenthesis and grouping together the characters that make our string.

```
[trevelyn@shell ~/regex]$ grep -E '(thisString)*' file.txt
Arkasia
Evol Intent
Camo and Krooked
thisStringmatches
thisString
matchthisStringtoanything4128850075
tttttthisStrin_doesnotmatch
[trevelyn@shell ~/regex]$ grep -E '(thisString)' file.txt
thisStringmatches
thisString
matchthisStringtoanything4128850075
[trevelyn@shell ~/regex]$
```

Listing 5.1.2: the glob-like zero-or-more quantifier in action.

In *listing 5.1.2* above,[17] we see that all results were returned when looking for the string "*thisString*". This is because it literally matched zero or more occurrences of the string.[18]

The zero or more quantifier is commonly used with the any character meta-character. For instance in *listing 5.1.3* we look for any word that starts with a 'c' and contains a 'w' anywhere after it.

---

[17] grep can also recognize strings without parenthesis when used alone.

[18] In Stephen Kleene's original mathematical definition of the '*' operator, he would specify sets as well, with {"i","gj"}* which would match **any combination** in **any amount** of the character 'i' and string "gj".

```
[trevelyn@shell ~]$ grep -E '^c.*w' /usr/share/dict/words |
head
cabbagewood
cabinetwork
cabinetworker
cabinetworking
cableway
caddow
cadew
cadweed
cagework
cahow
[trevelyn@shell ~]$
```

Listing 5.1.3: a common way of using the zero or many quantifier.

> ## Note!
>
> As for the shell, it doesn't work in this way. We have to shift our mode of thinking when using the asterisk as a quantifier in Regular Expressions. The glob, when used in UNIX shells, matches anything, but can before, after or even alone in commands. E.g. `ls *`, `ls A*`, `ls *B*`, etc.

Optional Quantifier

Another quantifier operator is the '?' symbol, which literally means that *"the previous character or set of characters is/are optional."* This character is also used in UNIX shells, albeit differently to mean *"any single character"* which may also confuse some new to regex syntax as this is not the case here.

```
[trevelyn@shell ~/regex]$ grep -E 's9?tru?angs?e' file.txt
very strange string
[trevelyn@shell ~/regex]$
```

Listing 5.2.0: using the quantifier operator for "optional" – being a single "?" symbol.

In *listing 5.2.0*, we test the strings with our new quantifier symbol '?'. This Regular Expression literally states *"search for an 's' followed by (either a '9' OR no '9') then a 't' then an 'r' then (either a 'u' OR no 'u') then an 'a' ... "* and well, we can gather the rest from there.

```
[trevelyn@shell ~/regex]$ grep -E 's ' file.txt
this line has spaces
this line has a nice space after the 's'
thislinehas a good space after the 's' too
[trevelyn@shell ~/regex]$ grep -E 's ?' file.txt
this line has spaces
thisline did not have a space
this line has a nice space after the 's'
thislinehas a good space after the 's' too
thislinehasnospacesbut one
[trevelyn@shell ~/regex]$
```

Listing 5.2.1: the optional operator is applied with the spacebar.

In *listing 5.2.1*, we see that we are trying to match a character 's' with a space after it, which returns three lines. The second command, states that the space is optional, which returns all lines with an 's' in them. Keeping in mind that this is a unary operator which acts upon a single operand and we defined this operator with a single character or set of characters, let's look at a set or string.

```
[trevelyn@shell ~/regex]$ cat file.txt
Gabriella hopped off of the couch!
get off there, rabbit!
[trevelyn@shell ~/regex]$ grep -E 'f (of )?the' file.txt
Gabriella hopped off of the couch!
get off there rabbit!
[trevelyn@shell ~/regex]$
```

Listing 5.2.2: some people don't like to use prepositions! Here we specify the string "of" is optional

In *listing 5.2.2*, we say that the string "of " (notice the space) is optional when just after an 'f and space. Always remember the quantifiers in Regular Expressions are unary and are not distributive.

One great use for this optional quantifier is for validating user inputted phone numbers. Some may put a hyphen '-', or period '.' between the NPA[19], local exchange and subscriber digits. Some people even put parenthesis around the NPA and some people use no symbols at all, just digits. How can we check for a valid phone number with a Regular Expression with all of these different ways of writing it out?

---

[19] Number Plan Area, or "Area Code" in the US

```
[trevelyn@shell ~/regex]$ grep -E '\(?[0-9][0-9][0-9]\)?[-
.]?[0-9][0-9][0-9][-.]?[0-9][0-9][0-9][0-9]' file.txt
412.555.1212
412-555-1212
4125551212
(412)555-1212
[trevelyn@shell ~/regex]$
```

Listing 5.2.3: a very looooong Regular Expression for validating phone numbers.

In *listing 5.2.3* above, we do just that! It is such a long way to do so though. Now, if only there was a way to say exactly how many occurrences of a digit from 0-9, then we could state *"3 for the NPA, 3 for the exchange, and 4 for the subscriber line digits."* Well, in Regular Expressions, there actually is a way, called the customizable quantifier that we will cover shortly!

Note!

We need to escape the parenthesis in this regexp or else the interpreter will think we are initiating a sequenced sub pattern! We want the parenthesis to be treated literally as expressed.

At Least One!

What if we wanted *"at least one"* result as a quantifier? Well, we have that with the "+" quantifier operator.

```
[trevelyn@shell ~/regex]$ grep -E 'r+' file.txt
very strange string
[trevelyn@shell ~/regex]$
```

Listing 5.3.0: the '+' quantifier operator in use.

Above in *listing 5.3.0*, we can see that our Regular Expression states *"at least one occurrence of the letter 'r"*. This Regular Expression "r+" matches "r","rr","rrr",..."rrrrrrrrr", etc. If we need to apply this operator to a string, we simply put parenthesis around the string.

Customizable Quantifier

One last quantifier we will cover is the most powerful. This was discussed in previous chapters and is the customizable range quantifier operator {n,m} which literally means "*at least n occurrences but no more than m occurrences of the previous character or expression.*" With this expression it is obvious that we can completely customize how many of what we want. This new quantifier is indeed the most powerful, but can also be the most confusing.

```
[trevelyn@shell ~/regex]$ tail -n 4 file.txt
sstring
ssstring
sssstring
ssssstring
[trevelyn@shell  ~/regex]$  tail  -n  4  file.txt  |  grep  -E
'^s{3,4}tr'
ssstring
sssstring
[trevelyn@shell  ~/regex]$  tail  -n  4  file.txt  |  grep  -E
's{3,4}tr'
ssstring
sssstring
ssssstring
[trevelyn@shell ~/regex]$
```

Listing 5.4.0: the fully customizable quantifier operator.

This new Regular Expression syntax as shown in *listing 5.4.0* first states "*match the beginning of the line and then an 's' character at least 3 times, but no more than 4, then a 't' and then an 'r'.*" Remember the anchor character '^' that meant "*beginning of the line*" from the previous sections? Well, we use it within this syntax because as we can see in the next statement we get a result that has 5 's' characters which technically would be out of our range of 3-4 otherwise. The reason for this is that it does match 4 's' characters then a 't', just with nowhere to start from! This is because this quantifier actually uses <u>OR</u> logic. For example, say we have the expression a{2,5} This literally states "*two 'a's <u>OR</u> 3 'a's <u>OR</u> 4 'a's <u>OR</u> 5 'a's.*"

```
[trevelyn@shell ~/regex]$ tail -n 4 file.txt
a sstring
a ssstring
a sssstring
a ssssstring
[trevelyn@shell ~/regex]$ tail -n 4 file.txt | grep -E 'a
s{3,4}tr'
a ssstring
a sssstring
[trevelyn@shell ~/regex]$
```

Listing 5.4.1: the fully customizable quantifier operator in a sentence.

This new example in *listing 5.4.1*, shows a simple example. A sentence "*a sstring*," doesn't match because our Regular Expression states "*an 'a' character followed by a space then at least 3 's' characters but no more than 4*"

Remember the optional quantifier character '?'? Since this means "*zero OR one of the previous character*" we can write this with the customizable quantifier also with {0,1} Our second quantifier "*at least one*" '+' can also be written with this as {1}. We can specify just one argument to the a{1} and this means "*exactly one 'a'*". If we have a{4} it means "*exactly four 'a's*".

Now we can recall our simple dilemma in 5.2.3 with repetition. Let's try the phone number Regular Expression with our new customizable quantifier syntax.

```
^\(?[0-9]{3}\)?[-.]?[0-9]{3}[-.]?[0-9]{4}$
```

Listing 5.4.2 our phone number pattern is much more compact using the quantifier modifier!

We saved a lot of typing with our new quantifier! And data de-duplication is what Regular Expressions are all about![20]

The customizable quantifier in Regular Expressions is extremely flexible and powerful. The syntactical rules for its usage are fairly easy to remember and we can use anchors to make sure that our strings are exactly in the form that we specified to the user for input.

---

[20] I really wanted to put a smiley face here.

Back References

This is yet another powerful addition to some Regular Expression powered applications. Back references allow us to preserve a matched character or set of characters for later use. These back references are created automatically by participating interpreter applications when we use the parenthesis to group objects and can be referenced by numbers. The numbers are variables that resolve to the value of exactly what was matched. Each application can handle back references differently and some applications don't even support them. Usually the variable name that holds our preserved text is a number that is escaped, or as in Perl, prefixed with a dollar symbol sigil '$'. Let's take a look at an example.

```
[trevelyn@shell ~]$ grep -E '([a-z])\1{2}'
/usr/share/dict/words
bossship
demigoddessship
goddessship
headmistressship
patronessship
wallless
whenceeer
[trevelyn@shell ~]$
```

Listing 6.1.0: back-referencing to find words with three of the same character in them.

Let's say we want to find words that contain three or more of the same character in them. In *listing 6.1.0* we do just that. We surround the character class for any alpha-character ('a' through 'z') in parenthesis. The Regular Expression interpreter assigns the first match to \1. Then it tests the next character as per the {3} rule we set and if it is the same character as the previous match, then it continues. If not, the interpreter knows that our Regular Expression match does not start at the first match's location and resets to the current location if and only if the current location is an alpha-character. This process is repeated until either the Regular Expression resolves as true or the interpreter reaches the end of the line. Without the use of the parenthesis and \1 variable, our pattern would be [a-z]{2} which would match any combination of any two alpha-characters, which is not what we are looking for.

```
[trevelyn@shell ~/regex]$ cat file.txt
Mississippi
[trevelyn@shell ~/regex]$ grep -E '((i)([a-z]){2})' file.txt
Mississippi
[trevelyn@shell ~/regex]$ grep -E '(([a-z])([a-z])\3){3}\2'
file.txt
Mississippi
[trevelyn@shell ~/regex]$
```
Listing 6.1.1: nested back-references order

We can nest back references. In *listing 6.1.1* we can see in our second example we matched the entire word except for the first letter, 'm'. We searched for any word that contains a three letter sequence three times. This sequence *"starts with any letter and ends with two identical letters,"* e.g. *"ipp","iss","off","goo"*, and so on. The first set of parenthesis that surrounds our entire expression is evaluated and assigned to \1. The second set, which is the first inner set around [a-z] is evaluated and assigned to \2. This method is great for finding specific unique usernames in files.

```
[trevelyn@shell ~/regex]$ grep '<[a-z "=:#0-9;]*>' file.html
<head>
<style>
<script>
<body>
<div class="lol">
<p>
<b>
[trevelyn@shell ~/regex]$ grep '<[a-z "=:#0-9;]*>' file.html
| sed -r -e 's/<([a-z]*) ?.*>/\1/'
head
style
script
body
div
p
b
[trevelyn@shell ~/regex]$
```
Listing 6.1.2: Back-referencing with sed for substitution.

In the above *listing 6.1.2*, we use back referencing to preserve strings in substitution. Our simple task is to compile a small list of all HTML tags used in a small markup page for our boss. First we use `grep` to find all HTML tags[21] that are not end tags; they do not contain the character '/' but can contain attributes e.g. `style="color:green"`. Next, we run the exact same command but pipe its output stream into `sed`. We then tell `sed` we are using Regular Expressions, and give it a single substitution command `'s/<([a-z]*) ?.*>/\1/'` In this regex pattern, we preserve only the first word within the angle brackets used to make the HTML tag.

---

[21] If the file were much larger we could even add a pipe to the sort –u command. This would load all lines into memory and print a unique list when completed.

Perl Regular Expressions

As previously stated, Perl's Regular Expression support is unbeatable. Perl's focus on text manipulation is just one reason why it is so popular in UNIX-like operating systems. This is because everything in a UNIX-like operating system is, or at least treated as, a file or *file descriptor*. Most of these files are static configuration files and dynamically generated output files for logs and device output. This is why we[22] consider Perl to be the best system administration tool. It can manipulate text, has a rich, comprehensive set of libraries, and is a full programming language. We assume that if you are reading this, you are slightly familiar with Perl, but we will construct full scripts in the examples. The first text manipulation function we will cover is simply matching text in the same filter manner as we used with grep in the previous chapters.

Matching Text

Matching text in Perl is incredibly easy. If we are reading log files from a UNIX server and we are looking for a particular string, say "*Text*" or "*txt*" we can use the **binding operator** =~ or the **smart match operator** ~~ within a clause and then the match function m//. The match function is similar to the grep filtering application and takes only one expression. This, of course, can be a simple string as well. We could simply search for lines that contain the pattern "*Text*" with m/Text/ or "*txt*" with the function called as m/txt/ but using Regular Expressions allows us to be more creative and powerful programmers. The match function can also have its own modifiers including case-insensitivity and *global* matching, m/Text/i and m/Text/g respectively. There are a huge amount of end modifiers we can use, in fact the

---

[22] WeakNetLabs.com

Perldoc[23] website includes m,s,i,x,p,o,d,u,a,l,g, and c as modifiers to the match function.

```
[trevelyn@shell ~/regex]$ cat file.txt
The Text file.
Did you receive my txt msg?
A line without the searched word.
Another great line that should go down in history.
[trevelyn@shell ~/regex]$ perl -e 'use warnings; use strict;
foreach(`cat file.txt`){print if($_ ~~ m/[Tt]e?xt/);}'
The Text file.
Did you receive my txt msg?
[trevelyn@shell ~/regex]$
```

Listing 7.1.0: Perl's Smart Match operator and the Regular Expression function m//.

In *listing 7.1.0*, we use the match function m// with the Regular Expression [Tt]e?xt and the Smart Match operator ~~ to print only lines that match our Regular Expression. If we add the capability to include arguments to this script for the file we want and the regex pattern, this script would act similar to grep but have the power to use Perl's Regular Expressions. This pattern searches for four words: "*Text,*" "*text,*" "*Txt,*" and "*txt.*" If we truly didn't care about upper or lower case, we could have simply used the regex pattern m/te?xt/i The search function can be used for anything that holds a literal string in Perl and we apply it to the $_ local variable which is assigned the next line as we got through *file.txt*

When used with a regex pattern, the matching function in Perl is one of its most useful text operations. Remember our example from the beginning of Chapter 1? Our very first regexp: ^--?h(elp)?$

We can easily implement this in Perl with the match function m//.

```
#!/usr/bin/perl -w
use strict;
print "Help: type words.\n" if($ARGV[0] =~ m/^--?h(elp)?$/);
```

Listing 7.1.1 Our very first regexp example from Chapter 1.

---

[23] http://perldoc.perl.org/

```
[trevelyn@shell ~]$ perl help.pl -h
Help: type words.
[trevelyn@shell ~]$ perl help.pl -help
Help: type words.
[trevelyn@shell ~]$ perl help.pl -h
Help: type words.
[trevelyn@shell ~]$ perl help.pl --h
Help: type words.
[trevelyn@shell ~]$ perl help.pl --he
[trevelyn@shell ~]$ perl help.pl --help
Help: type words.
[trevelyn@shell ~]$
```

Listing 7.1.2 Testing our very first regexp from Chapter 1.

Substituting text

Next, we will take a look at substituting text in Perl applications. We just showed how Perl's m// function is similar to grep. Well, Perl also has a substitution function s/// similar to sed. This function takes a regex pattern for its first argument and a literal, or a variable which contains a literal, for its second argument and looks exactly like a sed s/// substitution command.

```
[trevelyn@shell ~/regex]$ perl -e 'use warnings;use
strict;foreach (`cat file.txt`){$_=~s/[Tt]e?x[Tt]/TEXT/;
print};'
The TEXT file.
Did you receive my TEXT msg?
A line without the searched word.
Another great line that should go down in history.
[trevelyn@shell ~/regex]$
```

Listing 7.2.0: Perl's substitution command on the local variable $_

In the above *listing 7.2.0*, we have a simple Perl script which will print all lines after performing a substitution using the regex pattern [Tt]e?x[Tt]. The =~ operator is used once again to change the incoming lines that are assigned to $_ in order of being read from the cat command.

Back References can be used in the s/// substitution function. They are denoted with a sigil and an integer in order they appear to the

Perl interpreter. Instead of using \1, \2, \3, ..., etc as we do in sed, Perl uses $1, $2, $3, ..., etc as we see in *listing 7.2.1* below.

```
[trevelyn@shell ~/regex]$ perl -e 'use warnings;use
strict;foreach (`cat file.txt`){$_=~s/([Tt]e?x[Tt])/--$1--/;
print};'
The --Text-- file.
Did you receive my --txt-- msg?
A line without the searched word.
Another great line that should go down in history.
[trevelyn@shell ~/regex]$
```

Listing 7.2.1: Perl's substitution command using back-references

The substitution command also can have an end-modifier as well. The 'g' will perform the substitution for every occurrence of the matched pattern. Also, we can substitute the text and assign it directly to a variable without modifying the original using the 'r' character as we see in *listing 7.2.2* below.

```
[trevelyn@shell ~/regex]$ perl -e 'use warnings;use
strict;foreach (`cat file.txt`){$a = $_ =~ s/([Tt]e?x[Tt])/--
$1--/r; print $a.$_};'
The --Text-- file.
The Text file.
Did you receive my --txt-- msg?
Did you receive my txt msg?
A line without the searched word.
A line without the searched word.
Another great line that should go down in history.
Another great line that should go down in history.
[trevelyn@shell ~/regex]$
```

Listing 7.2.2: Perl's substitution command using the 'r' modifier to preserve the value in $_ .

Splitting Up Text

Now that we have looked at matching with the grep-like m// function and substituting text with the sed-like s/// function, let's look at just one more function similar to AWK for splitting up text. Just like in AWK, we can use a Regular Expression as a field separator as we did with -F in the chapter "AWK." This is done using the split(); function. The split function takes two arguments, the delimiter, or field separator, and a string to split up.

```
[trevelyn@shell ~/regex]$ perl -e 'use strict;use warnings;my
$string = "Hello1world2how3are4you?"; foreach(split(/[0-
9]/,$string)){print $_ . "\n";}'
Hello
world
how
are
you?
[trevelyn@shell ~/regex]$
```

Listing 7.3.0: splitting up text similar to AWK with any-digit [0-9] as a field separator, or delimiter.

In *listing 7.3.0* above, we split up the string "*Hello1world2how3are4you?*" and printed each field. These fields can be processed into a list and accessed individually also, which is very useful and similar to how AWK assigns each field to an integer, $1, $2, $3, ..., etc.

We can do this with `my @splitString = split(/regex/,$string);` and then access each field as `$splitString[0]`, `$splitString[1]`, ..., etc.

Note!

We need to be very careful when using Regular Expressions in Perl functions. This is because a variable can be used as a Regular Expression! This is considered pre-compiling an expression.

Precompiling a Regular Expression by mistake can lead to semantic errors in our programs when variables are used within pattern matching functions. For instance, if we create the variable `$regex` and assign to it the expression "*[Rr]egexp?*" we can then use that variable `$regex` in our functions and Perl will know that it is a Regular Expression.

Another way we can use variables in our Regular Expressions passed into pattern matching functions is with what's called interpolation. Interpolation takes the value of a variable and places that into a string of characters that could include literals or even more variables. An example would be if we assigned "*egex*" to $regex and then in our matching function we called it with m/[Rr]$regexp?/ This would give us an error stating that the global symbol "*regexp*" needs to be **explicitly defined**. Meaning that variable doesn't exist, even though $regex does.

```
[trevelyn@shell ~/regex]$ cat file.txt
A Regexp is a great tool!
A regex pattern is a great tool.
Regular Expressions are awesome!
[trevelyn@shell ~/regex]$ perl -e 'use strict;use warnings;my
$regex="[Rr]egexp?";foreach(`cat file.txt`){print if ($_ =~
m/$regex/);}'
A Regexp is a great tool!
A regex pattern is a great tool.
[trevelyn@shell ~/regex]$
```
Listing 7.3.0: Pre-compiling a Regular Expression in Perl

In *listing 7.3.0* above we pre-compile our expression. When a dollar sign sigil '$' is followed by other characters in a Regular Expression for a pattern function in Perl, Perl will check if a variable with the following name, in our case $regex exists before continuing.

Look-ahead Assertions

Perl's **look-ahead assertion** is great for showing lines that do not contain a specified string anywhere within them. They do as their title states and actually look-ahead from their current position for the pattern we choose. The syntax is simply a ?=regex within parenthesis.

```
[trevelyn@shell ~/regex]$ cat file.txt
Arkasia
Camo and Krooked
[trevelyn@shell ~/regex]$ perl -e 'my @l = `cat
fi*`;foreach(@l){print if ($_ =~ m/^(?!.*Kroo)/);}'
Arkasia
[trevelyn@shell ~/regex]$ perl -V
Summary of my perl5 (revision 5 version 14 subversion 2)
```
Listing 7.4.0: positive and negative look-ahead assertions in Regular Expression patterns to show and not show lines with specified strings.

In *listing 7.4.0* we first print all lines that contain the string "*Kroo*". Then we negate the look-ahead by changing the '=' character into a '!' and print all lines that do not contain the string "*Kroo*". We use the "*any character*" meta-character '.' And the asterisk "*zero or many*" quantifier to bypass any characters before the string "*Kroo*" These look-around assertions were introduced into Perl 5.

```
[trevelyn@shell ~/regex]$ cat file.txt
this line has a capital C in the middle of it.
C this line started with a capital c.
this line ends with a capital C
this line does not have any at all
neither does this line
[trevelyn@shell ~/regex]$ perl -e 'my @l = `cat
fi*`;foreach(@l){print if ($_ =~ m/^(?!C)/);}'
this line has a capital C in the middle of it.
this line ends with a capital C
this line does not have any at all
neither does this line
[trevelyn@shell ~/regex]$ perl -e 'my @l = `cat
fi*`;foreach(@l){print if ($_ =~ m/^(?!.*C)/);}'
this line does not have any at all
neither does this line
[trevelyn@shell ~/regex]$ perl -e 'my @l = `cat
fi*`;foreach(@l){print if ($_ =~ m/^(?!.*C$)/);}'
this line has a capital C in the middle of it.
C this line started with a capital c.
this line does not have any at all
neither does this line
[trevelyn@shell ~/regex]$
```

Listing 7.4.1 using negative look-aheads in Perl 5.

The first Perl command in listing *7.4.1* shows all lines that do not start with a capital 'C'. This is because the '^' before our look-ahead just before the parenthesis is the beginning line anchor. The second Perl command displays only lines that do not contain a 'C' at all. This is because of the "*zero or more*" quantifier used on the "*any character*" '.' Meta-character preceding the 'C'. This regex pattern literally means "*match any character at all unless is preceded by a 'C,' so look ahead for a 'C.*" The last command is the exact same but we added the end of the line '$' meta-character. This now states "*match any character at all unless is it precedes a capital 'C' that is at the end of the line.*"

It goes without saying that these look-ahead assertions in our Regular Expressions are extremely useful.

Regular Expression Examples

Email Addresses

Any application on the web should sanitize its user's input to avoid being attacked by XSS and SQL Injection. How can we make an expression that assures what the user inputs is only an email address and not HTML or PHP code?

```
^[A-Za-z0-9_.-]+@[A-Za-z0-9_.-]+\.[a-z]{2,4}
```
Listing 7.1.0: the large Regular Expression for email addresses

Looks pretty daunting, eh? *Well it shouldn't if you have read this far!* This is an example of a multi-ranged set. We included uppercase A-Z, lower case a-z all numbers 0-9, an underscore, period and ended the expression with a hyphen. We ended with the hyphen to not confuse the interpreter in use that it's trying to specify another range. Remember that all special meta-characters have no meaning in a range square brackets expression, so the period is just a period. We say we want at least one of these characters for what's referred to as the local name of the email address. Then we put in the symbol "@" and specify yet another multi-ranged set of character classes. This is the exact same as previously stated and used for the domain name of the email address. Again, we need at least one character. Then, we escape a period, since it is outside of the square brackets and is interpreted as "any character" if not escaped. Next is the ".com",".au",".info" top level domain portion of the email address. Note that this example uses no shortcuts and should be compatible with any up-to-date Regular Expression capable language.

Credit Cards

We know that the first number of a credit card is the major industry identifier. A credit card number that starts with a "4", for example, is from VISA and one that starts with a "5" is MasterCard. How can we tell if the credit card input from a user is VISA?

```
^4[0-9]{3}-?(([0-9]{4})-?){3}
```

Listing 7.2.0: A simple check for the first 4 digits in a line.

If *listing 7.2.0* returns true, then we know it is a VISA card number. We can see in *listing 7.2.1* that the regex pattern works using a simple cat and grep test command.

```
[trevelyn@shell ~/regex]$ echo 4123-1234-1234-1234 | grep -E
'^4[0-9]{3}-?(([0-9]{4})-?){3}'
4123-1234-1234-1234
[trevelyn@shell ~/regex]$ echo 4123123412341234 | grep -E
'^4[0-9]{3}-?(([0-9]{4})-?){3}'
4123123412341234
[trevelyn@shell ~/regex]$
```

Listing 7.2.1: Using the Credit Card check for VISA cards

We can take this search even deeper by figuring out the Issuer Identifier Number (IIN) account number and even checksum value.

```
IIN: ^[0-9]{6}
ACCT: 's/^[0-9]{6}([0-9]{9}).*/\1/'
Checksum: [0-9]$
```

Listing 7.2.1: A few Regular Expressions we can use to parse out information from the credit card number.

The first expression is simple: *"return the first 6 digits."* The second is a little more complex and we represent it within a substitution expression. We truncate the first 6 digits and drop the last digit leaving us with the account number of 9 digits. The last expression means give us the last number on the line which is the checksum used to calculate the validity of the VISA card number.

HTML

HTML tags are incredibly easy to spot and always start with a less than symbol '<' and end with a greater than symbol '>'. What's between and be a bit tricky. Some tags only contain alpha characters, for example "<pre>", "<body>", "<head>", ..., etc. while end tags will have a forward slash in them, for example "</pre>", "</body>", "</head>", ..., etc. Sometimes the tags will contain attributes, which means we will need to account for spaces, quotation marks, numbers, and equal symbols among others. If we are searching for a tag that has a Javascript function, we will need to include a semi-colon, parenthesis, and whatever else is used within the Javascript function. If our tag contains in-line styling, e.g. <span style="color:#000;">, then we need to add a hash symbol '#' and a colon as well. All of these examples can be seen in the listings below. The first, *listing 7.3.0* is all of the HTML code in the file.html file.

```
[trevelyn@shell ~/regex]$ cat file.html
<!DOCTYPE html>
<html>
<head>
</head>
<body>
        <div class="test">This is in the class "test"!</div>
        <br />
        <span
style="position:absolute;top:0px;left:0px;color:#fff;">HELLO!
</span>
         
        <pre>
                <code>
                        #!/usr/bin/perl -w
                </code>
        </pre>
</body>
</html>
```

Listing 7.3.0: the full file file.html

Let's find all tags with just alpha characters 'a' through 'z'.

```
[trevelyn@shell ~/regex]$ grep -E '<[a-z]+>' file.html
<html>
<head>
<body>
        <pre>
                <code>
[trevelyn@shell ~/regex]$
```

Listing 7.3.1: all HTML tags with just alpha characters

Now, let's accommodate for end tags.

```
[trevelyn@shell ~/regex]$ grep -E '<[a-z/]+>' file.html
<html>
<head>
</head>
<body>
        <div class="test">This is in the class "test"!</div>
        <span
style="position:absolute;top:0px;left:0px;color:#fff;">HELLO!
</span>
        <pre>
                <code>
                </code>
        </pre>
</body>
</html>
[trevelyn@shell ~/regex]$
```

Listing 7.3.2: all HTML tags with alpha characters and their corresponding end tags.

All we did was add a forward slash to the class. Now, let's find tags with attributes.

```
[trevelyn@shell ~/regex]$ grep -E '<[a-z]+ [a-z]+=".+">'
file.html
        <div class="test">This is in the class "test"!</div>
        <span
style="position:absolute;top:0px;left:0px;color:#fff;">HELLO!
</span>
[trevelyn@shell ~/regex]$
```

Listing 7.3.3: HTML tags with attributes.

In this regex pattern <[a-z]+ [a-z]+=".+"> we account for *"a tag that starts with at least one character followed by a space followed by at least one character and an equals symbol then at least one character within quotation marks."*

Searching for tags with javascript code in them can be a bit tricky. First we should realize that sometimes the code is within an attribute, such as onClick(); onMouseOver();, ..., etc. Sometimes it is just put after the onLoad attribute with a colon, e.g.

```
<body onLoad=javascript:alert("1337");>
```

Sometimes the programmer of the webpage won't use *camel-casing* to express functions and functional attributes. Camel-casing is when programmers concatenate words for variable and function names, but distinguish the words by capitalizing them all but the first. An example would be myNewFunction(); *Listing 7.3.4* is an example of how we can simply search for a function that has an argument surrounded by double quotes or single quotes. We also use a back-reference to simplify when deciding to end the argument with a double quote or single quote.

```
[trevelyn@shell ~/regex]$ grep -E '[a-z]\((["'\''])[a-
z]+\1\)' file.html
<body onLoad=javascript:alert("lol")>
<input type="submit" value="test button"\
onClick="alert('clicked');"/>
[trevelyn@shell ~/regex]$
```

Listing 7.3.4: Matching a function, in our case alert("test")

We can see that we needed to double escape the single quotes to avoid errors or interpretation by the shell. We create the Regular Expression pattern in the form '*regex*'\"*regex*' which is simply concatenating the two expressions with the single quote between.

Artificial Intelligence

Recently I began coding an IRC[24] bot in Perl. I wanted my bot to recognize that he or she had favorite musical bands that the bot would listen to. I wanted the bot to be as close to human as humanly possible. Completely strange and very odd, I understand, but follow along and I'll lead you to a beautiful regexp.

It's quite common to have social interactions with new folks in which we inquire about another's music tastes. So, I created a set of files in which the bot would read from with intrinsic names according to likes and dislikes. File names like bad_music.csv, good_music.csv, bad_foods.csv, good_foods.csv, etc. Well, when I realized there were many different ways I could ask her which bands she liked, I was presented with a Regular Expression puzzle.

Being human, we can use slang to change a sentence around. We can add profanity for exclamation, or leave out prepositions and other words. Sometimes it's best to do a string substitution to remove excess words before parsing with a regexp. But, there are always keywords in which help us understand what we are trying to say. To ask about what music bands another likes, there's a large number of ways we could go about doing so. In this example, I will only tackle a fraction of that, but by using a Regular Expression, I cut the cost of programming down significantly.

```
if($msg =~ m/^(do |did )?you ( ?ever )?(listen|hear|jam)( of
| to )?(the )?([a-z0-9_ *#@-]+)\?/i){
        # ... do stuff here
}
```

Listing 7.4.0: the most advanced Regular Expression in this manual.

There it is in all its glory. This expression will recognize many ways to ask a single question! I then parsed out the final word, or band

---

[24] Internet Relay Chat

name, as the sixth backreference. Here are eight different ways to ask about the band Rosebuds.

```
22:38 <@trevelyn> do you ever listen to the rosebuds?
22:38 < mina> yeah, i do
22:38 < mina> do you like Anakin?
22:38 <@trevelyn> do you ever jam to the rosebuds?
22:38 < mina> yeah, i do
22:38 < mina> do you like south central?
22:38 <@trevelyn> you ever jam to the rosebuds?
22:38 < mina> yeah, i do
22:38 < mina> do you like starflyer 0059?
22:38 <@trevelyn> do you listen to rosebuds?
22:39 < mina> yeah, i do
22:39 < mina> do you like sunny day real estate?
22:39 <@trevelyn> did you ever hear of the rosebuds?
22:39 < mina> yeah, i do
22:39 < mina> do you like Blue Sky Black Death?
22:40 <@trevelyn> did you ever jam to rosebuds?
22:40 < mina> yeah, i do
22:40 < mina> do you like south central?
22:40 <@trevelyn> you hear of rosebuds?
22:40 < mina> yeah, i do
22:40 < mina> do you like R.E.M.?
22:40 <@trevelyn> you listen to rosebuds?
22:40 < mina> yeah, i do
22:40 < mina> do you like Houses?
```

Listing 7.4.1 The bots actual responses to my question asked many different ways.

The entire Perl bot relies heavily on Regular Expressions which makes her return responses that are more human-like. I was able to create Purposeful typos and code for purposefully looking for typos as well.

Generalizing code with Regular Expressions makes it more flexible and ready for human error! If code can simulate human interaction this closely, it really makes one wonder how deep Regular Expressions can be in our everyday lives. If communication is such a large part of our lives, then how can Regular Expressions make what we do, not just in a programming sense, more efficient?

Contributing to Regular Expressions

My simple contribution to the science of pattern matching with Regular Expressions would be to implement negative backreferences for repeating sub patterns in the Regular Expression pattern itself. Because Regular Expressions are all about data de-duplication and compacting code as we have seen in this book, I propose that we implement a negative back reference to refer to a previously used sub pattern to minimize the length of long regexps. For instance, a backreference with an unsigned integer (positive number) returns the actual text that was matched.

```
#!/usr/bin/perl -w
use strict;
print $1."\n" if ($ARGV[0] =~ m/^([A-F]{3})[0-9]\1/);
```
Listing 8.1.0 example code that will print the backreferenced pattern.

```
[trevelyn@shell ~]$ perl negbackref.pl AFE5AFE
AFE
[trevelyn@shell ~]$ perl negbackref.pl AFE5AFF
[trevelyn@shell ~]$
```
Listing 8.1.1 output from the code in 8.1.0 which returns "AFE" as the backreferenced pattern.

The backreference \1 in *listing 8.1.0* becomes $1 and matches the string "AFE" in *listing 8.1.1*. This is why our second call with the altered first argument fails; "AFE" does not equal "AFF." But, what is we wanted to match [A-F]{3} twice? Why should we have to retype the sub pattern?[25]

Now, if we accept a regexp as input for finding a string, as $ARGV[1], we can parse the regexp and substitute negative numbered backreferences into corresponding sub patterns. Just as unsigned backreference go in order of appearance (\1 is the first set of parenthesis, \2 the second, and so on), negative backreferences would

---

[25] This is far more powerful when dealing with larger sub-patterns.

be the same in this respect (\-1 is the first sub pattern in parenthesis, \-2 the second sub pattern in the second set of parenthesis, and so on).

This may be a bit confusing, so let's try this in code, using only one sub pattern \-1.

```perl
#!/usr/bin/perl -w
use strict;
my $regexp = $ARGV[1]; # regexp
my $subreg = $1 if ($ARGV[1] =~ m/([\]\[a-z0-9]{\$+_:;"'><-
]+)/i);
$regexp =~ s/\\-1/($subreg)/;
print "true\n" if ($ARGV[0] =~ m/$regexp/i);
```
Listing 8.1.2

In *listing 8.1.1* I have coded the application to substitute all \-1 backreferences to the first sub pattern in the first set of parenthesis provided. Let's try it with the pattern ([A-F]{3})[0-9]\-1

```
[trevelyn@shell ~]$ perl negbackref.pl AFE5AFF '([A-F]{3})[0-
9]\-1'
true
[trevelyn@shell ~]$ perl negbackref.pl AFF5ECD '([A-F]{3})[0-
9]\-1'
true
[trevelyn@shell ~]$ perl negbackref.pl AFF5ECH '([A-F]{3})[0-
9]\-1'
[trevelyn@shell ~]$
```
Listing 8.1.3

In *listing 8.1.3*, I pass two arguments to the code written in *listing 8.1.2*. The first argument is the string in which I would like to search and the second is a regexp that will be manipulated before being applied to the pattern. As expected the pattern becomes ([A-F]{3})[0-9]([A-F]{3}) because the \-1 was changed to [A-F]{3} and then I wrap it in parenthesis during the substitution with the s/// function.

In changing the pattern, we saved 8 − 3 = 5 characters in the regexp. Now in the case of the phone numbers from, we can save even more.

In *listing 5.2.3* we have the regexp as,

```
^\(?[0-9][0-9][0-9]\)?[-.]?[0-9][0-9][0-9][-.]?[0-9][0-9][0-
9][0-9]$
```

without using a quantifier modifiers, which is whopping 69 characters. Then, in *listing 5.4.2*, we have the regexp as,

```
^\(?([0-9]{3})\)?[-.]?([0-9]{3})[-.]?([0-9]{3})[0-9]$
```

which shortened the code to 54 characters. Now if we apply the negative backreferences we can shorten this code even further to:

```
^([()]?)(([0-9]){3})\-1([-.]?)\-2\-4\-2\-3$
```

Now we have 44 characters! Not too shabby! Let's take a look at our negative backreference sequence patterns in order:

\-1	[()]?	Either a '(' or ')' is optional
\-2	([0-9]){3}	Three of any integers
\-3	[0-9]	(nested inside \-2) Any integer
\-4	[-.]?	Either a '.' or '-' is optional

Table 8.1.0 table showing our negative backreferences and the sub sequences the refer to.

In total we saved 69 − 44 = 25 characters. The beauty of negative backreferences is that they can be used with backreferences together to shorten code that has many repeating patterns. For instance, what if the NPA and exchange were the same in the phone number? Well, we can then shorten the code down to:

```
^([()]?)(([0-9]){3})\-1([-.]?)\2\-4\-2\-3$
```

Conclusion

Regular Expression syntax is a sub language that, when mastered, also requires us to fine tune our ability to recognize patterns. Eventually, it can significantly breakdown the amount of coding, scripting, pointing and clicking and even talking we do in our daily lives. This, along with a lot of other virtues can lead to wisdom.

Once we start using Regular Expressions on a daily basis, we can apply these simplicity principles to empower almost anything, not just code.

2014 WEAKNET LABORATORIES